SINLESS SOUL

THE VERSES OF LOVE

JANID KASHMIRI(AABID MAQBOOL)

ISBN 979-888546736-0

Contents

Contents

Contents

Preface

This book is a collection of poems written in the memory of beloved.

In this book, poet is expressing his love for his beloved (which he was unable to express before her).

The verses of this book are the verses of love and the voice of soul.

Love is about caring and protecting,

comforting and welcoming,

crying and smiling,

imagining and feeling.

It's about wanting and talking,

forgetting and remembering.

It's the love that is never ending and never stopping.

Come read and feel the emotions of a lover.

1. CAGE

The bird is in its cage,
It no longer laughs,
It no longer sings,
Its wings are worn from flying in this trap.
He imagines taking flight
Flying between the mountains,
Flying in the open sky,
Flying from sea to sea,
Rediscovery freedom was
Blinded without weapons.
Only misfortune was enough
Of an evil that has no face
And flying among them
As a great threat.
And I know that soon
It will show its wings again,
And will be lost in that sky
And will sing with the soul.

2. BODY OF CLAY

We are just a body of clay
And one day we will be dust
We bear so many sparkles
Arrogances that diluted
Because we are nothing,
We represent in this universe
I only found out that I am nothing
And you're also not what you think,
Simply that keep everyone
In Valued props that conquer apparent
Foolishness in a world of cowardice.
Let's go to the same place on different roads,
We are everything and we are nothing
Just dust and nothing else.

3. WHERE I AM

• 3 •

Where I am when I imagine justice
Hunting demons along side the saints?
Where I am when I recite the Daroodh
Raising my soul to the top?
Where I am digging up this poem?
Where is my heart sitting?
Can I perhaps inhibit another side
That is not where where my skin swing?
What is this curse that encourages me
To touch other space with my tongue
To see other figures and other lives,
To exist full in a lie
Demons are created when we divert
The brain only creates fantasies.

4. ARE YOU IN MY SOUL

I call your name in the empty night
I call for you in the cold dawn
Are you in my or in my dreams?
Because you make my days brighter.
I invite you and I wait for you
I want you to have your beating for me
I wish, but you are worth of wait
This love in my soul, in my heart has no end.
Come take me away from pain and loneliness
Come give me love at every time
Come bloom my days my sweet flower
Come love me with your soul.

5. INNOCENCE

You know, I should have warned my heart
I should have told it that nothing was serious.
Don't believe everything you told me
But no, I absorbed all the lie.
You know, I believed everything as a child
I was too naïve and innocent
I never spared the love I gave
I gave everything I had and was empty.
You know, with your actions you are
Achieving the miracle that I long for.
My heart is feeling less and less
Soon I will say goodbye to your world .

6. SINLESS SOUL

This is the story
Of a soul that was soon marked
From a young age,
He traveled a thousand worlds
Knowing hidden dimensions
Inadvertently
That his feet walked on this earth
Passing by with a vulgar appearance.
In his head, in his breathing, in his heart
The magic was shining, getting impossible
While your skin, your eyes
They withered
Well, little by little
He was distancing himself from his fellow men.
At first, he did not care
Well what I achieved,
It was more valuable than any happy memory.
In your dreams,
Nothing was unattainable
And so much discovery achieved,
It gave him the formula for any challenge.
Everything was perfect,
But suddenly, all that did not fill him

Something was missing inside
Something, that I would not fill
with any great achievement.
Never felt a warm caress
He never walked with his fingers across the sky
And realized
That all those successes,
far and near to equal parts
He had exchanged them for the truly magical.
So the pain took hold of him
With the only safe escape
Towards self-destruction based on toxins,
Alcohol, drugs, gambling …
I just wanted to fill that void
Inadvertently
That with every step, it was bigger.
He never quenched his thirst
And what at first relieved,
Came to force a fragile body
To depend on it.
So much so that it forced the machinery
To see if his heart would stop like that.
Today, it lives between everything and nothing
Not so valuable anymore
To keep breaking down unreachable walls
And of course, the only hugs that cover you
They are the ones who force

themselves to give themselves alone,
Ending night after night
With a single wish,
That when I die no one lies
And on your tombstone put
The Sinless soul who was never loved.

7. ECHOES OF MY SOUL

I embarked on an important journey
In search of your intense eyes,
Seeing the breadth of all eyes
In this wandering dream .
I found you in the empty spaces,
Hungry, thirsty and cold
At the behest of the heart,
The wind went in another direction.
Sadness gripped the belief
My senses and reasoning
In a very strange environment,
Tears were flowing with a lot of emotion .
I came across the waves to find you
At the new world as current did not allow
You to search for storms,
Thunders and hurricanes.
He made it difficult for us
To experience his love.
I found you in the sky,
The stars and the moon,
I found you inside me,
No matter what, the best thing

In life is to love you!

8. IN DARK

What power has that light
That manages my entire soul.
What power you have given them,
As they no longer want me to sleep.
Dark night that I feared
Without the light on your sidewalk,
Do not go my muse
Where you are.
Where is my sweet dream
Already of insomnia I am dying,
Because I love you so much
That without seeing you I despair.

9. WITH TIME THEY LEARN

In time they may know the truth

You can understand how impetuous life is,

Over time they adopts your philosophy,

On the way they can savor the fickleness

And prefer in life a sweet lie,

Before the harsh truth.

Understand why to put your hands in your pockets,

Staring at the floor and both shoulders slumped,

He also discovers that running in mud is not easy,

Discover that the fool is not always the lumberjack,

But the one who climbs the tree that will be cut down.

Over time they differentiates what is important,

What matters more where you are than where you've been

Just as courage is worth less than deed,

They realizes that crying is not cowardly,

You will also know that it is better that they shake hands,

So that they do not trample on the tulips

And discovers that love is the most powerful force

And that they must prove themselves in person,

Not in the coffin by laying roses,

That is what a person learns over time.

10. LOVE DOESN'T DIE

Love doesn't die
Or crumbs you must accept,
You must value it without
Letting yourself be trampled.
Love is a feeling of joy,
It is never from being hell
Or having insecurity.
They are beautiful moments
And even sad moments,
Sharing them, being two
When they really love you.
When are guises days is
When you see who is with you,
You see the true essence
Who appreciates you and who
From the back they stab you,
Leaving you aside with all their evil.
Do not let them impress you
Always be bold observing and
Observing until you
Always get to the truth.

11. THE LUCKY WIND

Now the wind travels through your neck,

I feel jealous why it is so easy for him to touch you,

I hardly speak to you and my mouth wants to leave the breath,

While I can only caress you with my eyes.

I trust that the moon will help me and convince you,

So that when you see you I no longer hear my gobble sound ,

I will look at you through the window, hug your pillow,

The dark night like my loneliness, will help me to enter,

Only then will my hand run through your beautiful complexion,

I hope you don't discover me between dreams,

But I would like you to dream me in one of them,

I dream of hugging you tight without letting go,

I want those our nights to be linked,

I am well lost in your garden of capulets,

I am looking for my Juliet in it

And I want you to be.

12. WHEN YOU LEAVE

If one day you go away,

Will you take with you the river of my tears?

If someday you go away,

Will you erase this pain in my chest,

The scratch with which you tore,

Deep my soul?

If one day you go away,

Will you give me back the light of my dawn,

The warm hope?

If one day you go away,

Free me from your memory,

From the sound of your name on my lips,

From the burning warmth that your hugs left.

If one day you go far away,

Do it at the end of dusk,

To believe you are just a dream, far away,

At the edge of the horizon, blurred.

If one day you go away,

A part of me will go with you,

And when on cold winter evenings you think of me,

You will understand what you've lost.

13. UNTRACEABLE PATH

I would like to walk on the path,

Without looking back,

So that the path I traveled

Cannot be retraced.

I would like Always keep going,

And no can never stop me ,

No matter how many difficulties

I may encounter on my way.

That life is just like

Walking and walking,

Crossing valleys and deserts,

To reach the end.

Without knowing if we will find,

Pain, or happiness.

That life is a draw.

What prize will we get?

14. I WILL WAIT FOR YOUR ARRIVAL

Sometimes I may be exhausted,

But I never renounce your gaze,

I wait for the day that will amaze me,

I await the day of your arrival.

Someday you will see how much I idolize you,

You will feel how much I try to touch your heart,

You will see my noble intention

And you will feel my unconditional love.

I don't want to be someone unknown

I want to be your faithful companion,

May my dreams be acts

And not from my mind a new deception.

Do not let me feel your absence,

Let me contemplate your beauty,

Empty the echoes of my soul,

And wander in the color of your perfect eyes.

I know I don't attract so much attention,

But I can assure you that I have good intentions.

15. HAPPINESS ~ A DREAM

Happiness is a bird
That learned to feed on leftovers,
Sleeping in any corner,
Drinking her tears
Like pure fresh water
To heal in silence, alone,
Thus challenging their bitterness,
Always pointing
Towards that infinite sky,
Taking flight in the rain.
Happiness is a bird
That survives every winter
Nesting under the shade
Of any smile,
Fleeing the cold of the anguish
That devours his existence
And lengthens his agony,
Fading during the summer,
Going unnoticed between
The superfluous joy
Of men who despise the miracles
That are brewing every day.

And we were little children
That they only played
Without dreaming of it,

Without wanting it,

Without wanting to stop
To contemplate it,

Without knowing,

That in our eyes

Photo the freedom

Of that innocent bird,

With its immense brightness
Was already being drawn.

Then we grew

And we saw Life

Setting fate traps
Wanting to find

Wanting to catch her,

With empty gestures,

False promises and words,
To be able to entangle it,

Becoming

In wretched blind men,

That having her in front
They could never enjoy it.

Now that I feel tired

I refuse to feed her,

I don't want to wait for her either,

My soul hurts
Just trying to imagine it,
Because it was me who
Destroyed its wings,
And could not keep it.
It is enough for me to know,
That I went through hell
To deserve my own peace,
My own calm,
Sometimes I thought
I saw happiness
Behind my window,
And I secretly smile,
Although I no longer have strength
For fake smile, for masked face.

16. EMPTY WE ARE

I see you struggling to get ahead,
To get out of bed with your spirits up
And the desire to laugh with others.
I see you looking lost
Trying to find your place.
Trying to travel to some better place
Where the emptiness is filled with love.
I see you looking for a place
Where you don't feel the same as today.
I see you trying to cover
Everything up to follow,
Feeling that you leave your backpack here
And you can fly free there.
And I know that from the emptiness
You're not going to get far,
The emptiness accompanies you,
As the emptiness is in you.
Emptiness is in everyone because
Emptiness is all trying to look in some corner
Everything we lack inside,
Trying to run fast to avoid
Taking it with us wherever we go,
I'm here to tell you that

Empty we are all, don't hurry,
Don't run trying to escape
Because without knowing,
What terrifies you goes with you
And doesn't leave you,
Come and sit down,
Let's clean our emptiness,
Put on music to make it more bearable,
Let's try to decorate it
So it doesn't look so dark,
Let's learn to go with it everywhere
Because empty we are all.
Come sit down, let's talk.
Let's start from scratch and
Stop looking for everything
We think we don't have.

17. AND I REGRET

My style is to walk as
If nothing was happening,
Knowing that an oversight will
Make me synonymous with oblivion,
Maybe I have something inside here
That cannot be explained,
Memories in my memory,
Dying of wanting to cry …
I regret it, and
I will only be happy.
When I can ask that girl for forgiveness
For being an idiot to her when
We left school I regret it,
Not being like the wind.
To have thought so much
About tomorrow, and tomorrow
And for thinking like that,
I miss millions of moments
I regret for
Not called you.
Every time I have thought
About leaving it and
Going out for you

To start doing everything.
I regret, daily,
Having failed you
For the nights when you cried
For everything I did.
Waiting for a hug
And a kiss and not being by your side.
It makes me angry
To know that I have never risked myself
I have been watching life go by
Instead of taking advantage
From the present,
I learned that now is a gift
I regret, of all my anger,
Of the merciless anxiety
That I spent arguing
With everyone for nothing.

18. LOVE THAT CROSSED MY AFFECTION

Love that crossed my affection
It left my garden without thorns
It filled my orchard with affection
It colored my life softly.
Hope emerged in my heart
Made the joy flow with more sensation
Even turned my winter into summer
My soul was filled with emotion.
Love that lit up my dawn
Made the sun shine brighter in the dawn
It took away the regret of my sunset
And the moon came out full in my night.
Love that fate brought to me
That made the rose bloom in the garden
The wind brought that endless longing
It's this Love that makes me happy like this.
Love that changed my story,
That showed, in life, a new trajectory
That made me reflect and think about victories,
It's this Love that I have eternalized in memory.

19. DREAMWORLD

I want to live in a sidereal world
Full of magic, stars and harmony
I want that goodness can conquer evil
And that children only have joy.
I want to live in a world without sadness
That there is no pain or crying
Where beauty reigns in the soul
Where the word is a sweet song.
I want to live in an imaginary world
Where we are all like brothers
Without death stalking us daily
Where we are immortal but human.
I want to live in a world of equality
Where evil or deceit does not reign
Fly with great wings of freedom
Leave behind the wounds and damages.

20. I OPEN MY HEART

There is a limit to the pain
But not for fear.
It is like hiding the fire
But not the smoke.
When the alarm sounds,
I want a day without leaving me.
When I say goodbye
It is not a goodbye,
I only alienate people with whom I do not
I feel good.
When I say I love you
It is not desperately,
But because I feel
That now I must say.
When I'm remembering
It is like when the waves
Arrive at the seashore,
They rest with less force
And that sound
He's so infatuated.
When I open my window,
I would like to see the sun, the moon,
The stars, the clouds, the rain,

And much more,
But not all this happens
In a single scene.
And when I say that I open my heart,
I open all the doors and windows to love,
And so it is that not everything
Happens in a single scene.

21. AND SHE LEFT MY HEART FULL OF HOPE

Again, she entered without warning!

She took up all the empty spaces,

She didn't ask permission to settle in

Like a sun when it warms up on a cold day…

She arrived with a charming smile

With open arms to soothe me

Piercing look, a provocative way

Wanting at all costs to fall in love….

She swore eternal love in the moonlight

She improvised verses for me to fall asleep

With blue rhymes like a starry sky

Said softly that he would never forget me…

She left my heart full of hope

She said it would be without a period and not even perhaps .

She took back our moments and memories,

It demarcated the whole scenario again.

22. YOU ARE THE REASON

Life is meaningful,
And in mine you are the reason
You are the one
I will love in the afterlife,
You are the one to whom
I dedicate this with my heart
From the moment I touched you,
The dark torment is gone,
I enjoy your charms
And your love of evil left me exempt
Those eyes, beautiful as the sea
And her long copper-colored hair
That's how life made her,
Impossible not to love
Dazzling in everything
Beautiful as a star,
And sorry if I exaggerate,
Beautiful like fall
I'm just sincere.

23. TEACH ME TO LIE

To deceive with the words
To pretend what not to be
In this world of shame
I will be your mentee.
Your outstanding student
I promise not to break
Any of your guidelines
I will let myself be sculpted
By deceptions and fallacies
Pretend that I am happy
On this battlefield
I will build a fortress
Certainly insurmountable
Where I will shelter my essence,
My fears and my truths,
I will be immune from comments
To unfounded judgments
From those who only want to
Sow doubts and harm.
So teach me to lie,
To deceive with words
I do not want to waste any more time
Exposed to the poison of fury.

24. TRACK OF TIME

I lost track of time!
The clock stopped ticking
I can't hear the whistle of the wind,
And the hours take a while…
Outside the time doesn't stop
I no longer control my simplicity
The imposed routine imprisons me
I'm going crazy for good.
I need to turn back time,
And let my watch work
Take a ride with the wind
I want to be free to fly and fly.
The stars start to twinkle
My soul is filled with emotion
Now I can have reason
I hear the rub_rub of my heart.

25. I WANT TO RUN AWAY

Why do I feel so bad?

Why doesn't life excited me?

Why do I feel alone amongst so many people?

I have no strength to move forward.

I've lost myself in my inner world

And I can't find myself.

I'm lost in some corner of my being,

Where there is no light,

I want to leave this world

Without making noise and

Traveling to the stars

Where I feel my real home is located.

I want to run away

From this state of life that so cruel

Treated me stealing

My dreams and freedom.

26. A LIMIT TO THE PAIN

There is a limit to the pain
But not for fear.
It is like hiding the fire
But not the smoke.
When the alarm sounds,
I want a day without leaving me.
When I say goodbye
It is not a goodbye,
I only estrangement people
With whom I do not feel good.
When I say I love you
It is not desperately,
But because I feel
That now I must say.
When I'm remembering
It is like when the waves
Arrive at the seashore,
They rest with less force
And that sound
He's so infatuated.
When I open my window,
I would like to see the sun, the moon,

The stars, the clouds, the rain,

And much more,

But not all this happens

In a single scene.

And when I say that I open my heart,

I open all the doors and windows to love,

And so it is that not everything

Happens in a single scene.

As time passes

It is being built or destroyed.

Maybe it's a matter of taste

In the eyes of the right person

Or from the wrong person,

You choose what you love

Or it chooses you

What you will come to love

Coming to feel that

I feel accompanied with myself.

And so there are limits,

But not to my imagination.

You can bear the pain in fear …

And not be afraid of pain.

27. A REBORN EXPRESSION

What my heart dictates to think of you
To think of how beautiful it is
To feel in this magic
That I don't know how to describe…
When thinking of you,
Emotions overcame me
All l think you only inhabit
letters of expression towards you
Reminding me that there is
no more beautiful inspiration than you
Thinking your smile is drawn in mine.
If I think in the distance I will be closer to you.
If you think me like me,
Then words have come to color
If you think me like I do,
Madness will invade your mind
If you think like me,
You will know that there is no verse,
No phrase I longed for waiting to see you
Our feeling will grow
If I have this desire to be with you right now,
It's because at night I have not stopped thinking about you,

I felt your voice near my ear,

Which is so thin and sweet that shudder my skin.

I don't know how you will manage to access my heart

If I didn't even give you the key.

Talking about feelings I always ended up

In a " I love you "

And there will always be something to join you..

Pass the time that passes,

Expressions are reborn in seconds.

What dictates my heart to think in you

It's something that keeps me alive emotionally.

Beautiful things are said

When you carry love in your heart,

In your essence.

It is the light in my path

And think alone reborn

The intense red color of my heart.

28. I WILL NEVER LET YOU FALL

Oh, how your sigh destroys me,

Voice sobs that trembles my ears,.

It subjects me to run to where you cry,

My soul doesn't allow me to leave you alone.

Your tears that fall to the floor,

It is a cold that hits my soul,

I do not mind nailing me here with you

And take your sorrows to oblivion.

Calming your pains is like a pleasure,

To please my instinct,

That is my goal,

He will never let you fall.

Chapter29

There is a space in my life
Where I miss you,
It is not a story of hugs
Nor story of tears ,
It's just from missing you
From the depths of a feeling
That does not get used to
That you are not.
It is not worth stopping time
Because I no longer remember
The moment I fell in love with you,
It was any day or any time,
It was a word or perhaps a gesture,
And I don't know if I loved you first
Or did I love you later
When I peek into the dark black
Of your eyes and I saw myself
Portrayed in them.

30. SOMETHING UNCERTAIN

There is something uncertain
That breaks me,
Something that traps me,
Something that destroys me.
A mirage, a confusion,
A product of my imagination.
You can't find the answers,
You don't have help,
Nothing is what it seems,
Even if everything looks like it.
And my mind alone suffers
A sweet and cruel torture,
Which condemns me to nonsense,
Leaving my heartbeat rendered.

31. A PERSON WITH GOLDEN HEART

Pure soul, that's what you are.

A person with golden heart ,

Worth a thousand smiles,

And the urge to hug you forever.

I get close to your precious calm,

Your goodness and

Your unfiltered eyes,

Which tear me through the abyss.

Every time I look at you,

It is incredible to discover you,

To understand that

You carry so much world inside,

And I, with so much desire.

My heart is in constant jump,

And your closeness,

The concern of wondering

If it is that perhaps,

Also jump to you,

The curiosity to burst the bubble.

Is the madness only mine?

32. BURNING FLAME

I can't tell what love is
To me it's a burning flame
And is good,
But hard sometimes.
It's very difficult when this same feeling,
Connects the wrong person
It's hard to let go
It's hard to love when this feeling isn't
Reciprocated
I wanted to learn
To command my feelings.
I'm happy anyway
Because my heart taught me
To know love.
There were times I regretted it
And there were times it enjoyed it
Nobody controls the heart,
It just happens Unintentionally.

33. MY VERSES

My verses are infinite
They are vulgar and affiliated
Are forgotten pieces
Collected by my own
And are whispers and screams
They are the doors
And are walls
And are last pieces,last voices.
My verses are vanities
Holes or halves
Jail and freedom
Full or half truth.
My verses are thorns
And are flowers without fragrance
They are fish on desert
In a desert of my heart.

34. AND I BELIEVE

I believe in deep glances,
In the language of caresses,
In the force of words
When the heart dictates them.
I believe in love as a cure
For the wounds of the soul.
I believe in the magic of a smile
And in the truth of a tear.
I believe in embracing life
Creating and collecting moments .
I believe in the sanity of the mad,
In the experience of the elderly,
In the innocence of children,
In the hands of my mother.

35. SOMEDAY I PROMISE MYSELF

I would like to stop having feelings

And freeze the heart

Stop trusting one hundred percent

And just say goodbye

I would like to

Leave this world

To leave a mark

Let it sink deep

I would like to see

The shine in your eyes

And a big smile

Caused by me

But none of that

Will be happening

I still feel

I'm still living

It still hurts

I keep crying

Someday I promise myself

To stop feeling

The good, the bad and the ugly

And live in peace.

36. BRIGHTNESS OF DAWN

The brightness of dawn
Came and no one woke up,
Because that shine only belonged to you,
That's when you showed up.
And I saw you.
And underground we heard
The singing of birds.
The sky blue dyed pure white
And the world totally
Stopped for a second.
And I heard you,
From deep inside.

37. PALE DREAMS

• 47 •

The pale dreams fly over my soul,
In the dark hours only pain keeps my company.
Thoughts tear apart the reality that is confused
With abstract and terrible feelings.
In the abyss of uncertain hours
Where peace runs away from the soul
And calm runs away from me.
I bleed and crying out loud.
I feel a void of sunny days
Where life was throbbing and full of colorful dreams.
Today only pain of my being follows me
Where I go like a horrible shadow.

38. WOUNDED SOUL

You laugh
With open wounds.
Your eyes are
A couple of broken stars
Where the crying sprouts
Over a deserted valley.
You live in a hole
That no one else observes,
Nothing will stop,
Everything will remain the same
Between the forgotten drawers,
From the bottom of the abyss
Always encouraging those
Who are afraid of falling.
The darkness devours you
In a corner of your room,
The same corner
Where you sit alone,
And write bunch of poems.
You give love without feeling loved
You comfort without being comforted.
You die slowly in a world
Without being heard.

39. FRIENDSHIP

The time is here, it's there
Here and now
Loose laughter, tight hug , small talk
Happy music, crying on the shoulder.
It's like this, it's roasted
It's feeling, allowing, learning.
Moment is what remains,
The longing that beats.
It is the heart that asks,
Measures, and feels.
It's the sincerity of friendship
That speaks with nothing to say.
Unique moments in the memory
That remains in a heart that overflows.
Eternal moments of life,
With Sincere friends.

40. WHEN LOVE ARRIVES

When love arrives

It does not care about the barriers,

It does not care about the chains,

It does not care that you oppose it

Because it comes

And runs over you.

When love arrives

It invades us with desire,

Invades us with warmth,

Invades our desire from head to toe

Uncontrollable feeling even

Of the most immense emptiness

Turning everything upside down

And returning everything to its place.

41. WOUNDS AND SCARS

Wounds and scars
I have and you have.
They heal
Or they remain.
They show what we are
And what we live.
Some are small,
Some are big
That cannot be explained,
Because the lumps in the throat
Do not let you speak.
Others teach you and
You learn all the days of them.
And there are those
That do not mean anything,
But are part of you.
They all are whether
You like it or not.

42. I AM A HUMAN BEING

I usually hide my emotions,
But that doesn't mean
That I don't have feelings.
That you never see me crying
Doesn't imply that
I do not do it inside.
But I also cry I also feel.
I also need your caresses,
Of your sleepless nights.
Generally always
I feel good,
Sometimes not,
But normaly
You don't realize
I live my sorrows in silence
And my tiredness.
My love
I'm not doing
A reproach,
I just want you to know
That I am also
A human being,

Despite to be a Man.

43. HEART IN LOVE

Heart in love,

Smile on face.

That feeling of being happy at all times.

Brilliant eyes.

Distracted mind

But think of that someone.

Everything is related to you.

Music was never so my favorite.

How I learned so many romantic songs.

Because I sing these songs.

It's all happiness in me.

I'm dying to see you again.

I recently had you company

But I miss you already.

This emotion overwhelms me totally.

I needed to come to you.

And hug you tightly.

Heart in love and I can't focus,

My mind just keeps remembering you,

Because I have no other hobby to think about,

Because that's how I feel more alive,

I am falling in love.

And this love covers me completely,

By your side I want to be close
I want to feel alive.

44. IT'S OKAY TO WALK AWAY

It's okay to walk away
And be able to understand
Who accompanies your actions
And wants to see you bloom
It's okay that one day
You can just pretend
That someone can hug you
To the bones of yesterday
And hope that another story
Go rolling to start
And understand that
There are moments
In which you don't give anymore
It's ok to lay down
In soft flowers and see
How the great roof recedes
With nothing else to do
It's okay that one night
Put your mind off
And don't keep planning
Everything around you
It's okay to take care of yourself

Or that you let yourself
Be taken care of
It's ok if you do
Just to start over.

45. I AM NOT DIFFICULT TO LOVE

They told me so many times

That I am someone difficult to love.

And I began to believe too,

That it was true.

I told others that

I am impossible to treat

Don't waste your time,

And look for someone else .

They have made me feel that

If I wanted something,

It was something volatile ,

And that if something bothered me

I shouldn't have said it.

Now I understand that

I am not at all difficult to love.

Only they didn't make an effort

To understand me.

And then they blamed me

For not being able to understand.

From now on I will not feel anymore,

That I am difficult to love.

Now I will say that being by my side okay

But you have to win that place.

46. EMPOWER YOURSELF

Empower yourself
Because you are going to need it
Give yourself courage in every rhyme
When you find yourself alone
Give yourself time some night
To simply slow down
Take a while on the sidewalk
Sitting with a beer in hand,
Waiting for nothing
Give yourself life in every step
Give yourself strength to walk
Give yourself some time to be sad
Without knowing what will happen
Give yourself love, if that love
Own that you are still fighting.
That self love, once and for all
Give yourself a lot of laughs
Get angry, but for a while
And then I was you again
Realize betrayals
Give yourself a new chance
Give yourself necessary duels

To be able to move on

Give yourself nothing,

Give yourself everything

But give it without hesitation

Because everything you find

No one else is going to give it to you

Because life has the value that you give it.

47. FIND ME AND LOST ME

Find me and
Lost me again.
Watching and listening,
Crying,
The laughs
The noises,
The eternal nights,
The endless days.
Going through the scars
A thousand times.
Seeing how the old wounds
Reopened and feeling
The seed of many learnings
That began to flourish.
Thousands of chrysalis,
Turned butterflies,
The chest full of wings, of resurgence.
They were days on a calendar,
They were just days,
Which became months.

48. INCOMPLETE STORY

I think you are some
incomplete story of mine,
I feel the taste of your love.
Explain with your eyes what you have done
Why my heart melted in tears?
I left the time in your desire,
Why are you tormented even in my love?
You are the one who asked
my mistake in front of me.
If I wept, why you wept with me.